Atchison, Topeka and Santa Fe Railway

VOLUME 1

Vanishing Vistas®   BY RICHARD E. COX

Cover illustration: **The Grand Canyon** at Lemont, Illinois.

Inquiries should be directed to Vanishing Vistas, P.O. Box 15902, Sacramento, California 95852-0902. Telephone: 916-929-3855

Printed in the United States of America.

ISBN 0-912935-00-6

Santa Fe Railway Photo

Some measure of motive power progress on the Atchison, Topeka & Santa Fe Railway over the span of half-a-century can be discerned by noting that a 2-8-0, very much like the one in this photograph, was the heaviest locomotive in service on the railroad in 1879, yet in that time span would become the lightest one capable of road duties. That early engine, carrying its water supply in a saddle tank and its coal bin attached to the cab, weighed 115,000 pounds, an utterly unbelievable amount at the time. But that locomotive, then claimed to be the world's largest, was a very special one, having been built to pull and push trains over Raton Pass astride the Colorado-New Mexico boundary while a tunnel was being bored beneath the ridge.

By the next year, 1880, the 2-8-0 type was fast on its way to becoming the standard mainline freight power on the Santa Fe, and one of them, No. 132 built by Baldwin in 1880 (construction number 5266), was destined to become famous through its restoration and preservation as a memento of the railroad's early history. The locomotive, together with two ancient wooden coaches, is kept at the Topeka, Kansas, shops and is exhibited whenever an appropriate commemoration would be enhanced by its appearance. One of these occasions took place at Ponca City, Oklahoma, about 1950, where this photograph was taken of the venerable machine and its cars. The reconstruction was very well executed, and the locomotive resembled its builder's photograph with remarkable fidelity, though there were a few details which could not be practically reproduced.

When number 132 was delivered it weighed 110,000 pounds, of which 96,000 pounds were carried on its 50 inch driving wheels. Its cylinders were 20 x 28 inches, and its steam pressure was 140 psi.; its tiny grate had an area of only 27 sq. ft. Since the Santa Fe's main line in Colorado and New Mexico was characterized by a number of grades in excess of 3%, many locomotives, including the 132, were equipped with Le Chatelier water brakes.

The engine was renumbered 912 in 1898, then became No. 2414 in 1900. Three years later, when the Santa Fe received its first 2-8-2's, the 2-8-0's days were numbered. The 2414 was demoted to yard switching service, as were its existing companions. Meanwhile, some rebuilding had taken place. Its smokebox had been extended, and it had lost its huge stack and headlight. Its crosshead and guides had been changed, and its cylinders were altered to 19 x 28 inches, with 51 inch drivers. In 1926 the 2414 was still in service, though it had been converted to an 0-8-0 type, by removal of its pilot truck, for further use as a shop-switcher at Argentine Yards, Kansas. The next change in its appearance came when its rectangular tender was replaced by a slope-back one.

In 1940 the engine was retired from active service and given a diamond stack, large headlight and horizontal-bar pilot for historical display. But its modern tender betrayed the historical illusion, despite the initials of the present-day railroad's ancestor: A.T. & S.F.R.R. (the R.R. became Ry. around the turn of the century). So, back to the shops went the 2414. When it emerged after this most recent metamorphosis, it was numbered "1" and named **Cyrus K. Holliday** after the founder of the Atchison & Topeka Railroad. (The railroads first engine had in fact been so named, though it was not a 2-8-0.) Evidence of modernity had been camouflaged by appropriate decoration and embellishment, and the restored locomotive was entirely worthy of the Santa Fe Railway.

Vanishing Vistas®

Illustration: 2-8-0 No. 1
         Cyrus K. Holliday
Location: Ponca City, Oklahoma
Photo date: Circa 1950

ATCHISON, TOPEKA AND SANTA FE RAILWAY

SANTA FE RAILWAY PHOTO—TEXT BY ROBERT A. LE MASSENA

Photo by Bill Pennington

On most railroads a 4-6-2 doubleheading a 4-8-2 would have been followed by a long heavy passenger train; but this was not necessarily so on the Atchison, Topeka & Santa Fe, which in many ways was an unusual railroad. It had 2-10-4's with 74 inch driving wheels and a 65 mph. speed limit. It preferred B-B diesel-electric units for its fastest passenger trains; and 4-6-2's, 4-8-2's, 2-6-2's, and 4-8-4's worked in freight service. In California's almost-level great Central Valley, during the late-1940's, it was commonplace for 4-6-2's and 4-8-2's to handle freight between Richmond on San Francisco Bay and Bakersfield at the northern foot of Tehachapi Pass, a distance of 300 miles. These engines, displaced from mainline passenger service by 4-8-4's and internal-combustion units, were ideal power for freight duties where gradients were not demanding.

Although the valley of the San Joaquin River is gently inclined, rising only 400 feet between its mouth and Bakersfield, the Santa Fe experienced some difficulty with the terrain between Richmond and Antioch where the Sacramento and San Joaquin rivers join together in the upper-bay area. The Southern Pacific had occupied the strategic strip of shore on the southern side of Carquinez Strait, forcing the AT&SF system to find another location inland when the San Francisco & San Joaquin railroad (a Santa Fe subsidiary) in 1900 built 70 miles of track between Stockton and Ferry Point to give the system a terminal on the eastern shore of San Francisco Bay. The SF&SJ's rails headed away from the shore of Suisun Bay just east of the strait at Port Chicago, and climbed two ridges before returning to water level at Pinole, eight miles north of Richmond. Eighteen miles in length, this route across the intervening ridges involved two tunnels and a long steel trestle. The longer tunnel was 1.3 miles long under Franklin Ridge, and Glen Frazer, at its western portal, marked the end of an eight-mile ascent from Pinole.

As a type, the 4-6-2 was fifteen years older than the 4-8-2, the first two of which had arrived in 1918. A couple-hundred 4-6-2's had been acquired from the Baldwin Locomotive Works between 1903 and 1913, and when the 4-8-2's appeared, after a period of five years when no 4-6-2's had been purchased, the end of the 4-6-2 was a reasonable prediction. Commencing in 1919 and ending in 1923, the AT&SF added forty-nine more 4-8-2's (numbered 3702 - 3750), all from Baldwin. Surprisingly, then, the Santa Fe ordered more 4-6-2's from Baldwin in 1919, and procured fifty more of them through 1924, numbered 3400 - 3449.

Intended primarily for heavy passenger service on the mainline between La Junta (Colorado) and Los Angeles, the 4-8-2's supplemented the 4-6-2's which were assigned generally between La Junta and Chicago, where the grades were relatively light. Excepting minor variations in weights, which ranged from 339,000 pounds to 395,000 pounds, the 4-8-2's were all virtually identical. They had 69 inch driving wheels, and 28 x 28 inch cylinders. With their original steam-pressure of 200 psi. they exerted a tractive effort of 54,000 pounds, and 60,000 pounds when the pressure was raised to 220 psi. The first 22 engines burned coal on 72 sq. ft. grates, and 16 tons were carried in the tender along with 12,000 gallons of water. The tender rode on two six-wheel trucks, and weighed 243,000 pounds (loaded).

The 4-6-2 closely resembled the 4-8-2's mechanically, and they had identical tenders. The 3400's burned oil (4000 gallons in the tender's tank) in a firebox with only 3 sq. ft. less combustion area. Steam pressure and cylinder stroke were the same, also, but 25 inch diameter cylinders and 73 inch driving wheels produced a tractive effort of only 41,000 pounds. The engine alone weighed 312,000 pounds. All but a few (3409, 3443 - 3445, 3449) of the 3400's were changed to 220 psi. pressure and 79 inch drivers, but those five engines retained their original wheel-diameter, and were used between La Junta and Denver, then later in California.

Vanishing Vistas®

Illustration: 4-6-2 No. 3444 /
                 4-8-2 No. 3703
Location: Glen Frazer, California
Photo date: 1948

ATCHISON, TOPEKA AND SANTA FE RAILWAY

PHOTO BY BILL PENNINGTON—TEXT BY ROBERT A. LE MASSENA

TA-005-1-1470:

Photo by James L. Ehernberger

In 1930, the Lima Locomotive and Baldwin Locomotive companies constructed remarkably large 2-10-4's of similar dimensions. The forty engines built by Lima for the Chesapeake and Ohio were intended to replace 2-8-8-2's in heavy coal-train service, while the lone engine for the Atchison, Topeka & Santa Fe had been designed to supersede the 2-10-2 as that railroad's mainline freight locomotive. Consequently, the Santa Fe's version had slightly larger cylinders (30 x 34 inch) and drivers (69 inch). Though their grate areas were identical (122 sq. ft.), the Baldwin design had a higher steam pressure (300 psi.) and a somewhat smaller boiler (100 inch diameter). Tractive efforts were the same (93,000 lbs.), but the C&O engine weighed a bit more than the AT&SF's 502,000-lb. total. The Santa Fe's tender was smaller also, carrying 27 tons of coal and 20,000 gallons of water.

The C&O purchased no more of that wheel arrangement, and for a period of eight years neither did the AT&SF, a prolonged business depression having been the primary reason. However, the next ten (numbered 5001 - 5010) greatly surpassed all others of that type. Alone, the engine weighed 545,000 lbs. Its boiler had been enlarged to 104-inch diameter, and though the grate area had not been increased, the steam pressure was raised to 310-psi., thus yielding the same tractive effort with 74-inch driving wheels. The tender, riding on two six-wheel trucks, held 21,000 gallons of water and 23 tons of coal (5001 - 5005) or 7000 gallons of oil fuel (5006 - 5010), and weighed 360,000 lbs. The mechanical design followed AT&SF standards generally, but surprisingly, roller bearings were not applied to any axle.

The new locomotives were put to work hauling fast freight trains over the low-grade line between Kansas City (Kansas) and Belen (New Mexico) which had only one major summit at Mountainair (New Mexico), 39 miles east of Belen atop a ridge at 6470 ft. elevation and nearly 1700 ft. above Belen on the Rio Grande River. Despite their obvious success, more of them were not immediately ordered. The rising tide of World War II traffic brought great numbers of four-unit diesel-electric locomotives to handle freight and passenger trains on the more mountainous western portions of the Santa Fe's system, and the railroad discarded plans to replace its 2-10-2's with 2-10-4's. However, wartime traffic required still more motive power, and a final group of 25 locomotives was purchased from Baldwin in 1944. Improved versions of previous ones, they were numbered 5011 - 5035 (construction numbers 70817 - 70851).

Compared to the previous ten, the new locomotives embodied several modifications, while retaining the one-piece cast-steel bed, Worthington feedwater heater, and two forward-mounted compound air-pumps. Roller bearings were applied to all axles of engine and tender, the latter supported by two eight-wheel Buckeye-pattern trucks. The pilot truck was changed to inside-bearing arrangement, and Boxpok-design driving-wheel centers replaced the Baldwin type. Walschaerts valve-motion was still used, but the Laird 2-guide crossheads were replaced with single-guide construction. All of these locomotives burned oil, 7000 gallons of which, plus 25,000 gallons of water, having been carried in the tender. The loaded tender weighed an enormous 460,000 lbs., the engine itself having been about 7000 pounds lighter.

The 5021, pictured here in helper service out of Belen, operated for the last time in August 1957. Not scrapped, this fine example of a steam locomotive remains in storage at the time of this writing in 1973.

Illustration: 2-10-4 No. 5021
Location: Near Abo, New Mexico
Photo date: July 1, 1956

ATCHISON, TOPEKA AND SANTA FE RAILWAY

PHOTO BY JAMES L. EHERNBERGER—TEXT BY ROBERT A. LE MASSENA

Photo by Charles H. Kerrigan

The gas-electric, with its flat face, sharp cracking exhaust, and a sometimes whiplash ride, performed an important role in the development of modern railroading. Commonly called "doodlebug," "puddlejumper," "pop-car," they served the countryside in a variety of capacities: as Railway Post Office and Mail Car, Railway Express Agency, and passenger transport.

The 1910-1918 years saw the emergence, patronage, and downfall of the first gas-electric railcar era. General Electric pioneered the theme and built some eighty-five cars during the period, but the technology was a little too advanced for those times. Mysteries of internal-combustion, generators, traction motors, and associated control equipment became an unwanted headache for the railroads. By 1918 most of the first generation gas-electric railcars were either scrapped or put into storage. However, their period of dormancy was not to be a long one.

Shortly after the beginning of the roarin' twenties, branch lines quickly began losing money to an increasing competition of buses, flivvers, and trucks. When operating figures showed that the doodlebug fitted the 1920's as snugly as a piston in a cylinder, railcars started upon a renewed career of popularity—not of esthetics, but of utility. Fifty cents-a-mile doodlebugs versus the $1.25-a-mile branch line steam train represented a considerable savings.

A newly formed company took the lead this second time around: The Electro-Motive Engineering Company—EMC—later to become a part of the Electro-Motive Division of General Motors. EMC delivered its pioneer gas-electric in 1924, and by 1931 the EMC nameplate was on some five-hundred doodlebugs, or about eighty-percent of all gas-electrics built during their second era. For the most part, gas-electric construction came to pass when the great financial depression collapsed the railcar market. Even though the gas-electric itself was lacking in appearance, they were the vanguard of such handsome internal-combustion units as those of the **Rockets** and **Zephyrs, Super Chief** and **City of San Francisco**.

The Santa Fe M.154, pausing here at Cherryvale, Kansas, with a trailer coach, is an Electro-Motive product of June 1931. This 75 foot combination Railway Post Office-baggage unit was originally powered by a 400-horsepower Winton gasoline engine, but late in 1948 the M.154 was converted to diesel power for the remainder of its service time. Railcars of many brands, styles, and types rolled over the vast Santa Fe system. Beginning with the M.100, a McKeen car delivered in 1909, the Santa Fe Railway eventually operated a total of fifty-six railcars, thirty-seven being of the EMC brand.

The M.154's daily duty commenced at 7:45 AM at Coffeyville in southeastern Kansas. At Cherryvale, 27 miles to the north, it turned to the west, and covered 90 more miles to reach Winfield on the Santa Fe's north-south mainline into Texas. Then, heading northwesterly, it passed through Wichita and reached Newton on the east-west mainline at 12:55 PM, having traveled 174 miles. After allowing 2 hours and 20 minutes for lunch and servicing, the motor train (as it was called in timetables) retraced its circuitous route, and tied up in Coffeyville at 8:40 PM. During its journey, the train bore four numbers: 114 - 13 - 14 and 13 - 14 - 113.

Vanishing
Vistas®

Illustration: EMC No. M.154
Location:　Cherryvale, Kansas
Photo date: November 26, 1946

ATCHISON, TOPEKA AND SANTA FE RAILWAY

PHOTOGRAPH & TEXT BY CHARLES H. KERRIGAN

TA-005-1-1167:

Photo by William H. Mills

The great mountain barrier which extends thousands of miles along the Pacific Ocean offers very few easy routes of access to the country beyond. The states of Oregon and Washington share one such avenue, the Columbia River Valley, but California, with approximately 1000 miles of coast, possesses none. Consequently, that state's railroads (Southern Pacific, Union Pacific, Santa Fe) were forced to ascend extremely steep grades whose western feet are only a few miles from the sea. The Los Angeles metropolitan area, in particular, is severely handicapped in this respect. Four end-to-end mountain ranges with peaks exceeding 10,000 feet elevation, separate the coastal region from the vast high desert lands to the east. The San Gabriel Mountains lie directly north of Los Angeles, and since a corporate ancestor of today's Southern Pacific had occupied 3230 foot Soledad Pass to the west, lines constructed later would be thus obligated to use 3820 foot high Cajon Pass at the eastern end of the range, where the San Bernardino Mountains begin.

Despite its disadvantages, there was no doubt that Cajon Pass would be used by the Atchison, Topeka & Santa Fe railroad which was extending its transportation empire westward across Arizona in the early 1880's. In the meantime, the Southern California railroad, one of the Santa Fe's ancestral companies, had built a line between National City, on the ocean 100 miles southeast of Los Angeles, and San Bernardino, 50 miles east of Los Angeles at the foot of Cajon Pass. The SC laid track up the steep southern approach to the pass, then northeastward into the Mojave Desert as far as Barstow, 80 miles from San Bernardino. Two other construction subsidiaries of the AT&SF completed a connecting line between Los Angeles and San Bernardino, and by 1887 Santa Fe trains were operating between Chicago and Los Angeles.

The original line up Cajon Pass was incredibly steep; the summit was nearly 2000 feet higher than San Bernardino, and the track distance between them was only 25 miles. Much of the grade was 2.3%, but the final seven miles to the top were 3.5%. It was not the only such gradient on the Santa Fe's mainline, however; the approaches to Glorieta Pass in New Mexico and to Raton Pass in New Mexico and Colorado were equally steep, as well as longer. Because of the immense volume of traffic flowing through Cajon Pass, the AT&SF experimented with some very large locomotives to reduce the number of helpers moving up and down the hill. It tried a pair of Baldwin compound 2-8-8-2's, four home-made 2-8-8-0's constructed from existing 2-8-0's, and ten 2-10-10-2's made from 2-10-2's plus new low-pressure front sections. The Baldwin engines were fairly successful, but the other articulateds proved inadequate for the task, and they were taken apart and restored to ordinary 2-8-0's and 2-10-2's. Eventually the Santa Fe settled on the 2-10-2 for a universal road locomotive and helper, and purchased them by the hundreds from the Baldwin Locomotive Works. The 3882 was delivered in 1924 and bore construction number 23578.

For three decades the ponderous 2-10-2's reigned supreme on the grades of Cajon Pass, even after a 2.3% grade second track had been built for uphill traffic in 1913. But, when the GM-EMD FT-model four-unit diesel-electric locomotive was accepted by the Santa Fe just before World War II, the aging steamers were doomed, although it was not until 1954 that the last of them vanished from the Cajon Pass grades. During the War the AT&SF purchased these B-B units with 1350-horsepower engines as fast as they could be assembled, starting their numbers with 100, 100A, 100B, 100C, of which the center two units were boosters. The 412, with construction number 2602, had been built as the 147C in 1945, while the 412A, with construction number 2252, had been delivered as the 147B in 1944.

Vanishing Vistas®

Illustration: EMD FT No. 412 /
              2-10-2 No. 3882
Location: Cajon Pass, California
Photo date: June 1950

ATCHISON, TOPEKA AND SANTA FE RAILWAY

PHOTO BY WILLIAM H. MILLS—TEXT BY ROBERT A. LE MASSENA

TA-005-1-1859:

Santa Fe Railway Photo

The original profile of the Atchison, Topeka & Santa Fe accounts to a major degree for the railroad's choice of motive power. About half of the more than 2000 miles between Chicago and Los Angeles were located on the Great Plains where gradients were gentle with the only short steeper stretches, none of which exceeded 1%. The remainder, through a corner of Colorado, northwestern New Mexico, central Arizona, and Southern California, was an operational nightmare. From La Junta the rails ascended almost 3000 feet to Raton Tunnel, then dropped over 1500 feet beyond it. The approach grades were 3.5% and 3.3%, respectively. Glorieta Pass, almost as high as Raton, was attacked from the east by a 1.7% grade, and on the west by one of 3.0%. It was 2500 feet down to Albuquerque, then right back up again to the Continental Divide east of Gallup, with long 1% grades on both slopes of the watershed. Another 2500 feet was lost coasting down to Winslow, and the grade was 1.4% in places going up the 2500 foot climb to Flagstaff. From there the tracks dropped 6800 feet to the Colorado River at Needles, with adverse grades reaching 1.8% west of Seligman and 2.6% east of there. Another 2000 foot up-and-down summit was surmounted into Bagdad, whence the rails climbed 3000 feet to Cajon Pass on a 1.5% maximum grade, after which they slid down the 3% incline almost 4000 feet to the Pacific Ocean.

Santa Fe locomotives consisted of two varieties: those which produced power at very low speeds, and those which produced it at very high speeds. Two other factors were involved: water became scarcer the farther one receded from Chicago, much of which was unsuited to locomotive boilers without treatment: and, oil was more available than coal. The outcome of these basic facts-of-life was a roster of steam locomotives which surpassed all others for peculiar variety. The Santa Fe possessed more compounds, articulated and otherwise, than any other railroad, the result of the desire for fuel and water economy. Almost everything on wheels was compounded by one scheme or another: 2-6-0's, 2-8-0's, 2-10-0's, 2-6-2's, 2-10-2's, 4-6-0's, 4-8-0's, 4-4-2's, 4-6-2's, 2-6-6-2's, 2-8-8-2's, 2-10-10-2's, and 4-4-6-2's. The Santa Fe experimented with 2-6-6-2's having jointed boilers, and it spliced existing 2-10-2's to new 2-10-0 machinery to create not-very successful 2-10-10-2's. What wasn't compounded was monstrous, and it would be difficult to dispute the assertion that AT&SF 4-6-4's, 4-8-4's, and 2-10-4's were the most powerful of their types, and capable of making a 2000 mile run without attention other than water, fuel, and lubricant.

Prior to World War II, Santa Fe mainline power had been concentrated in just a few types: 4-6-2, 4-6-4, 2-8-2, 4-8-4, 2-10-2, and 2-10-4. Within their operating territory they could handle anything at any speed. Meanwhile, the diesel-electric streamlined passenger train had made its debut, and Santa Fe motive power people were aware of the characteristics of its locomotives: no water, low fuel consumption, and power at both high and low speeds. Very quickly they learned that standard GM-EMD FT-models were capable of handling both freight and passenger runs, and the end of the steam era on the AT&SF was then just a matter of time. In this picture, new 4-unit FT passenger locomotive 160 and freight haulers 119 and 113 pose in front of the new Barstow Diesel Shop. EMD F3-model 21, and a single set of Alco PA's number 57L, A, B complete the scene.

Vanishing Vistas®

Location: Barstow, California
Photo date: Circa 1948

ATCHISON, TOPEKA AND SANTA FE RAILWAY

SANTA FE RAILWAY PHOTO—TEXT BY ROBERT A. LE MASSENA

TA-005-1-179:

Santa Fe Railway Photo

Less than a year old, Santa Fe Alco passenger set number 56 makes a rare appearance on the famed **Super Chief** as it heads eastbound across the monumental Canyon Diablo bridge and straight into the morning sun. It is the spring of 1948, and the streamlined, all-Pullman train has only been in daily service for a couple of months. The Alco appearance is rare because they were mainly used on secondary runs. They were originally purchased for service on the prime trains, but couldn't hold up on the tight schedules and were quickly replaced by modified F3 and F7 freight units from rival builder EMD.

Canyon Diablo, twenty-seven miles west of Winslow (Arizona), was first bridged by the Atlantic and Pacific railroad in 1882. The A&P, jointly owned by the Santa Fe and the Frisco, built Santa Fe's original line west from Albuquerque (New Mexico), across Arizona to the Colorado River at Needles (California), where connection was made with a Southern Pacific line from Mojave (later sold to the Santa Fe). The line became an actual part of the Santa Fe in 1902. Winslow was reached in November 1881, and then six months were required to bridge Canyon Diablo. The first bridge, a spidery single track affair, was 560 feet long and 225 feet high.

Despite the age of the route, the bridge in this picture is less than a year old. To meet the demands of steadily mounting traffic, Santa Fe built the present double-track steel cantilever bridge in 1947. It is 544 feet long with a 300 foot center span, and it is the highest bridge on the system, with the railhead 223 feet above the canyon below. It was built massive to allow for heavier loads in the future and to eliminate the need for speed restrictions. Today the **Super Chief** paused to pose for this picture, but normally it would flash by without slackening from the maximum allowable ninety miles-per-hour. The bridge opened for operation on September 11, 1947, and the first train across it was eastbound number 4, the steam-powered, all heavyweight **California Limited**. At the left of the picture can be seen the stone and concrete footings of the deck-girder viaduct that the present bridge replaced.

The all-Pullman **Super Chief**, the pride of Santa Fe's passenger fleet, was inaugurated in Chicago on May 12, 1936. It was a special consist of up-graded **Chief** cars pulled by one of EMC's (predecessor to EMD) first road diesels, Santa Fe numbers 1 and 1A. This train established the long standard 39 hour and 45 minute schedule on the 2227-mile Chicago-Los Angeles run and made one round trip a week. This special heavyweight consist was only a temporary arrangement, however, set up to prepare the way for an all-new streamlined train under construction by the Budd Company in Philadelphia.

The new streamlined **Super Chief** departed Chicago on its maiden journey on May 18, 1937. It was one of the most luxurious trains ever to appear in the world. It was an immediate success, and Santa Fe promptly ordered more new streamlined equipment to increase the capacity of the train. On February 22, 1938, a second full train was inaugurated, and the **Super Chief** began operating twice a week in each direction. On the same date, the new all-coach streamliner **El Capitan** made its appearance as a companion to the **Super Chief** and the famous **Chief** was streamlined. After the war, more streamlined cars were delivered, and on September 29, 1946, the **Super Chief** began operating every other day, alternating with the **El Capitan**. Then finally, on February 29, 1948, the **Super Chief** was placed in daily operation, still running on a "39 and 45" schedule (which was later cut to 39½ hours). In 1950 and 1951 the train was completely re-equipped, at which time the now famous Turquoise Room-Pleasure Dome lounge cars were introduced. Although the operation of the train was consolidated with the **El Capitan** in 1958, the **Super Chief** is still first-class in every way, and in 1970 is unquestionably the finest train in the country.

Vanishing Vistas®

Illustration: **The Super Chief,**
      eastbound
Location: Canyon Diablo,
      Arizona
Photo date: 1948

ATCHISON, TOPEKA AND SANTA FE RAILWAY

SANTA FE RAILWAY PHOTO—TEXT BY RICHARD WILSON

TA-005-1-3618:

If someone wanted to see the big Alco PA/PB-series passenger diesel-electrics in action, his chances were best in the southwestern quarter of the nation. They were found on the Union Pacific, Missouri Pacific, Texas & Pacific, Denver & Rio Grande Western, Texas & New Orleans, Southern Pacific, and Atchison, Topeka & Santa Fe systems. These last two railroads possessed the two most extensive fleets of the units in the country, with those on the Santa Fe totaling 44, all PA/PB-1 models acquired over a short two year period. The first ones, cab-booster-cab set number 51, debuted in September 1946, as Alco's 75,000th locomotive. Eleven more three-unit sets soon followed, numbered 52 thru 62. The individual units were designated "L" (for "lead," and the letter was never visually applied), "A" (the PB booster unit) and "B." This created confusion with the trailing cab units, however, since Santa Fe's many EMD F-series freight units were in four-unit sets with "L-A-B-C" designations, and the letter "B" was already commonly identified with booster units. As a result, the trailing PA cab units were redesignated with the letter "C" to conform to the established pattern, giving the Alco sets an "L-A-C" identity.

The designation problem was soon moot. The balance of Santa Fe's Alco fleet was a quartet of cab-booster pairs, numbered 70 thru 73. At the same time they were being acquired, the Santa Fe separated the trailing cab units of the earlier sets and renumbered them in May 1949, as single units 63L thru 69L and 74L thru 78L, giving the fleet a final make-up of sixteen cab-booster pairs and twelve single cab units. They could then be operated in any combination of one to four units. (Single unit No. 63L was renumbered back to 51C when the original three unit set was sent to EMD to be re-engined in 1954.) No. 69, leading two other Alco units in this portrait of the **Grand Canyon** at Lemont, Illinois, was originally the 57B, produced in 1947 (construction number 74689).

The **Grand Canyon**, a leisurely train which in its earlier years stopped for meals at Fred Harvey's dining rooms along its route, departed Chicago's unreconstructed Dearborn Station at 11:00 AM and rolled through Lemont, 25 miles out, at 11:38 AM. As this picture indicates, the track was straight and level; it was also fast, and mile-a-minute plus speeds were the rule rather than the exception. The **Grand Canyon** was not destined to be known for its overall speed across the favorable profile through Illinois, however, as the train was obligated to stop for local passengers at 38 flag-stops in that state, in addition to the four scheduled ones. No speed records were to be broken in Missouri either; 22 stops were scheduled prior to its 8:50 PM arrival in Kansas City. At Trinidad, Colorado, helpers were added for the 17 mile climb up the 3.5% grade to the tunnel under Raton Pass, but the Alco's (and EMD A1A-A1A units also) were left to ascend the 1.8% grade of Glorieta Pass unassisted. Before reaching the end of its journey in Los Angeles, three more 1.5% gradients were encountered, all negotiated without help. Arrival at the Los Angeles Union Passenger Terminal was specified for 12:10 PM, making the overall time 51 hours, 10 minutes for the 2224 mile trip, a respectable performance in view of the local traffic handled on the train.

The **Grand Canyon's** consist underwent considerable alteration en route. A 24-duplex roomette car was added at Kansas City, and a chair car and 6-section/6-roomette/4-double bedroom sleeper (both originating in Dallas) were cut in at Winslow, Arizona. The Pullman lounge car, 8-section/2-compartment/2-double bedroom sleeper, dining car, and other chair cars made the entire trip from Chicago to Los Angeles. In earlier years, some of the sleepers had been cut out at Williams, Arizona, for a side trip to the rim of the train's namesake Grand Canyon.

^{TM}

Vanishing Vistas®

Illustration: **The Grand Canyon,**
                westbound
Location: Lemont, Illinois
Photo date: Circa 1959

ATCHISON, TOPEKA AND SANTA FE RAILWAY

TA-005-1-1540:

Santa Fe Railway Photo

The Atchison, Topeka & Santa Fe's 2227 mile mainline run between Los Angeles and Chicago had long stretches where 100 mph. speeds were attained by the railroad's fastest passenger and mail trains. But that trackage also included some short and extremely steep gradients of 1.4% to 3.5% which could slow diesel-electric traction motors to burn-out speeds. It was on these grades that the low-speed B-B unit with a 1500-hp. engine demonstrated its superiority over the high-speed A1A-A1A with 2000 engine-horsepower. In a sense, all of the B-B's quarter-million pound weight was utilized in producing power, while the idle axles of the heavier A1A-A1A contributed nothing useful at low speeds. Consequently, GM-EMD F-series models, from FT- through F9-, some of them converted from freight to passenger duties, powered most of Santa Fe's passenger train fleet following World War II. Toward the end of the 1950-decade, C-C units of higher power (2400 engine-horsepower) became available, and they began to replace the aging B-B units. With no unpowered axles, each of the new C-C units was the equivalent of 1½ B-B units on a weight-power-tractive effort basis of comparison. Typical contemporary examples were RSD-15 models from Alco, SD24 models produced by GM-EMD, and the GE U28CG model.

These initial developments were just the beginnings of dramatic increases in single-unit power capabilities made during the late 1950's and continuing throughout the 1960's. Two examples were GM-EMD SD24 No. 924, and Alco RSD-15 No. 822. Both locomotives are pictured here in front of the Barstow (California) diesel shops shortly after delivery in 1959. The AT&SF received 80 of the SD24 model, numbered 900 - 979, in 1959 - 1960. In contrast, 50 RSD-15 models were received during the same time period, numbered 800 - 849. In the renumbering at the end of the 1960-decade, in which similar units were grouped together, the GM-EMD SD24's and Alco RSD-15's became 4500 - 4579 and 9800 - 9849 respectively. The paint scheme applied to both models at time of delivery was the short lived black with silver safety stripes.

The Santa Fe's route through the arid country of the nation's southwestern quadrant was well suited to the introduction of diesel-electric motive power. In this region of little rainfall and meager fuel supply, water was poor and scarce, and coal or oil were hauled long distances. Other contributing factors were four summits with steep grades on both sides, which required one or two helpers on both freight and passenger trains. Diesel-electric units could be operated in multiple, thus eliminating helpers as well as providing adequate power at high operating speeds. Moreover, their thermal efficiency was so much higher than steam power that they could carry adequate fuel for extended runs without having to stop for replenishment, to say naught of the elimination of water stops. Thus, they were a logical solution to the railroad's operational problems.

Barstow, situated in the center of California's southern desert, is the junction of two lines which serve the state's two largest cities. Los Angeles is 137 miles distant, to the southwest, beyond Cajon Pass with its 1.6% (east side) and 2.2% (west side) gradients. San Francisco, 461 miles to the northwest, requires trains to surmount Tehachapi Pass, whose gradients are 2.5% (west side) and 2.3% (east side). Hence, Barstow is a very logical turnaround point for the Santa Fe's largest locomotives, as well as for the introduction of new ones in freight service.

Vanishing
Vistas®

Illustration: EMD SD24 No. 294 /
              Alco RSD-15 No. 822
Location: Barstow, California
Photo date: 1959

ATCHISON, TOPEKA AND SANTA FE RAILWAY

SANTA FE RAILWAY PHOTO BY DON ERB—TEXT BY ROBERT A. LE MASSENA

Santa Fe Railway Photo

The Atchison, Topeka & Santa Fe's **Super Chief**, though introduced at a time when steam locomotives were close to their ultimate development, was a creation of the internal-combustion motive-power age. Its original consist of standard cars was pulled by the railroad's first diesel-electric road-service locomotive, a pair of B-B units, each housing two 900-hp. engines. Just a year later its propulsion was supplied by an equally powerful combination of cab-and-booster units riding on A1A-A1A trucks, two of GM-EMC's earliest E1-models. In subsequent years, as the train's makeup increased, E3- and E6-models, both with 2000 engine-horsepower, were found at the head end, but steam helpers were still needed on the 3% to 3.5% grades over Cajon, Glorieta and Raton passes. After World War II, Alco A1A-A1A units of 2000 engine-horsepower in three-unit groups were used to propel the **Super Chief**. However, they were soon displaced by combinations of four GM-EMD F-series models (some of which had been hastily converted from freight duties) because of their superior performance in the lower speed range. On the occasion of this photograph the **Super Chief's** motive power consisted of four F3-model units, the first and last being cab units; the two middle ones were boosters, with train-heating equipment. The 30, 30A, 30B, 30C were received by the AT&SF in 1948-49 just ahead of the improved F7-models. Motive power of these two types continued to haul the Santa Fe's finest passenger trains until the mid-1960's, when they were superseded by high-power C-C units.

Instead of experimenting with lightweight streamlined articulated trains, as did other railroads in those days, the AT&SF first tested a pair of diesel-electric units which could be coupled to any existing assemblage of passenger equipment. Then, after having been satisfied on such matters as reliability, the railroad boldly inaugurated a new deluxe high-speed train pulled by these embryonic versions of internal-combustion locomotion. The six-car formation, composed of renovated heavyweight cars and timed for a 55½ mph. overall average speed, could have been handled nicely by one of the 4-6-4's, but the eight powered axles of the diesel-electrics gave them a decided advantage during acceleration and low-speed hill climbing where the steam locomotive would have required a helper. Then, too, the new kind of power needed almost no water, and it could carry fuel sufficient for long distances without a stop.

By mid-1937 the **Super Chief's** old retinue had been converted to a seven-car formation comprised of new lightweight cars produced by Budd, and new motive power also. The fast schedule and luxurious appointments attracted so much new patronage that another set of cars was ordered for a second train, which provided twice-weekly service between Los Angeles and Chicago beginning in early 1938. Since the **Super Chief** catered only to a sleeping car clientele, the all-coach **El Capitan** was added at the same time, running on the same days (leave Los Angeles on Tuesday and Friday; leave Chicago on Tuesday and Saturday) and on the same timing (less than 40 hours). After World War II the AT&SF, like other western railroads, expanded its passenger services, placing the **Super Chief** and **El Capitan** on an alternate-day schedule, and in early-1948 both were operated daily. During 1950 and 1951 the **Super Chief** received completely new cars, including the sumptuous "Pleasure Dome" dining-lounge-observation cars which incorporated the private "Turquoise Room" beneath the domed area. The train in this picture was one of that era.

In this scene, the **Super Chief** is running eastbound near Thoreau (New Mexico). Located just a few miles east of the Continental Divide, Thoreau is situated 129 miles west of Albuquerque and 32 miles east of Gallup. Train time for No. 18 at this location was about 11:20 AM.

Vanishing Vistas®

Illustration: **The Super Chief,**
         eastbound
Location: Near Thoreau,
         New Mexico
Photo date: Circa 1951

ATCHISON, TOPEKA AND SANTA FE RAILWAY

SANTA FE RAILWAY PHOTO—TEXT BY ROBERT A. LE MASSENA

Santa Fe Railway Photo

Passengers aboard the eastbound **Chief** of the Atchison, Topeka & Santa Fe railroad passed through three times as many tunnels in the course of their lengthy journey between Los Angeles and Chicago as passengers aboard the westbound train. Prior to 1909 the only tunnel on the entire mainline was a single bore under Raton Pass in northern New Mexico. In that year a second tunnel was completed beneath the pass, and thereafter eastbound trains used the old tunnel, while westbound consists went through the new one. Then, in 1913, something happened which added two more tunnels to the eastward route, but none to that headed west.

Both of these new tunnels, one of which is shown in this picture, were located in Southern California on a new segment of track laid on the southern flank of Cajon Pass north of San Bernardino. Ever since the rails were extended over the pass in 1886, a single track had carried the traffic of the Santa Fe system. Union Pacific system trains began to use that same line in 1905, under a trackage agreement, and as traffic increased the pass became a major bottleneck to both railroads. The difficulty was not so much the single track, but the steepness of the gradient. The top of the pass was almost half-a-mile higher than San Bernardino, although only 17 miles distant on the map. The rail route followed the only practical approach along Cajon Creek, and even though it took 25 rail-miles to do so, much of the gradient was 2.3%, and the final five miles was close to an incredible 3.5%, like that of Raton Pass.

Passenger trains presented little problem; they were not heavy nor were there enough of them to cause congestion. Heavy freight trains were the root of the trouble. They crawled up the grade at snail speed, occupying the track for far too long a time, and multipled helpers were visible testimony to the operational handicap imposed by the hill. The Union Pacific met the challenge with 2-10-2's and 2-8-8-0's. The Santa Fe tried much the same formula, using 2-10-2's, a couple of Baldwin 2-8-8-2's, and some 2-8-8-0's and 2-10-10-2's constructed in the company shops. Since the last two kinds of compound articulateds had been fabricated from existing 2-8-0's or 2-10-2's with new front sections, they lacked adequate grate area, and consequently the big locomotives just ran out of steam. After only two years of service their inadequacies became so apparent that in 1913 the Santa Fe installed a second track around the steepest portion of the grade, and relied thereafter on 2-10-2's to hoist its freight up the hill.

Between San Bernardino and Cajon station the second track was laid right alongside the existing one, forming standard double track. Above Cajon, however, the second track diverged to the west on a new route to avoid the stretch of 3.5% on the original line. This new line, stretching for nine miles between Cajon and Summit (compared to seven on the original line), held the uphill grade to 2.3%, the same as below Cajon. The two tunnels, each about 500 feet long were located on this new line; they pierced two ridges a quarter-mile apart at approximately the mid-point of the line, and they were virtually invisible from the older alignment, which was thereafter used only for westbound downhill movements. In this picture, the eastbound **Chief** is about to enter the lower tunnel.

Diesel-electric unit No. 302 was originally the lead unit of locomotive 302, 302A, 302B, a cab-booster-booster combination of F7 models built by GM-EMD in 1949 (construction numbers 8714, 8722, 8723). Supplementing a group of 21 four-unit F3 model locomotives received between 1946 and 1949, the F7 models were coupled in both four-unit and three-unit assemblages, the latter receiving road-numbers in the 300-series. These two classes of diesel-electric power, comprised of units having B-B trucks and 1500-horsepower engines, effected the transition from steam power in Santa Fe passenger service, and they ruled the line for two decades before being themselves retired or supplemented by more advanced locomotives of considerably higher engine output.

Vanishing Vistas®

Illustration: **The Chief**, eastbound
Location: Alray, California
Photo date: Circa 1960

ATCHISON, TOPEKA AND SANTA FE RAILWAY

SANTA FE RAILWAY PHOTO—TEXT BY ROBERT A. LE MASSENA

Photo by Chard L. Walker

Travelers on Santa Fe passenger trains between Los Angeles and Chicago could say that their journeys were not exactly alike, at least insofar as tunnels were concerned. On the eastbound trip two tunnels were encountered close to the top of Cajon Pass in California, and another was situated under Raton Pass just south of the Colorado-New Mexico border. Because there were two bores at Raton Pass, westbound trains passed through a different tunnel, but when they rolled downhill from Cajon Pass they used a completely different track, bypassing the tunnels on the uphill line. In this picture the eastbound **Chief** is at the east end of Alray siding, entering the upper tunnel on the climb toward the summit of Cajon Pass on March 20, 1950. (The downhill track is out of sight, far to the right.)

The **Chief** had departed Los Angeles Union Passenger Terminal at 12:30 PM, and passed the little wooden depot on top of the pass at about 3:00 PM. At 1:55 PM the next afternoon it paused at Raton (New Mexico), before ascending the pass north of the town. On the following day, after racing across 1000 miles of prairie, the **Chief** came to rest in Chicago's Dearborn Station at 11:30 AM, completing its 2226 mile journey in just 45 hours. In the opposite direction the **Chief's** schedule called for a Chicago departure at 1:30 PM, and it began its climb up Raton Pass from Trinidad (Colorado) at 8:00 AM the next morning. It was about 6:00 AM the second morning out when the train reached Cajon Pass, and it arrived in Los Angeles at 8:30 AM.

The **Chief** had its birth in the opulent mid-1920's, when railroad travel was the land equivalent of steamship transport on the oceans. It could be described in no better way than this direct quotation from a contemporary full-page advertisement in the Official Railway Guide: "A miracle of travel luxury—built for those who like their life on a train to have the refinement of home. Valet, barber, ladies' maid, bath, ladies' lounge, and observation sunparlor are part of the **Chief's** equipment. Fred Harvey Club and Dining Car Service sets the standard in the travel-world. The **Chief** is a sensation—a demon for speed! Slips smoothly over half a continent in two business days—Chicago to Los Angeles! Extra fast, Extra fine, Extra fare." By "extra fast" the Santa Fe meant a 6:00 PM departure from Los Angeles and an 11:00 AM arrival in Chicago, with an elapsed time of 63 hours. By "extra fine" the railroad offered unusually luxurious (for the time) non-air conditioned, heavyweight sleeping cars providing sections, drawing rooms, and compartment accommodations. And "extra fare" was translated as ten dollars.

A quarter-century later the extra fare was still $10, but 18 hours had been subtracted from the overall timing. In the interim, the **Chief** had been streamlined in 1938 and dieselized in 1946. Its standard of luxury had been scrupulously maintained, however. No fewer than three lounges were provided, one occupying an entire car adjacent to the diner, one located in the rear-end observation car visible here (which offered four-drawing rooms, and a double bedroom also) and one in the head-end car which also accommodated the train's service staff at night plus some incidental baggage. The rest of the cars in the **Chief's** make-up were sleepers, offering a full range of sections, roomettes, double bedrooms, compartments, and drawing rooms. (Coaches were not added to the train until the mid-1950's.) Three of the sleepers ran thru to the eastern seaboard, two to New York City (via the NYC and PRR) and one to Washington, D.C. (via the B&O), while the rest originated and terminated in Chicago. One of the Chicago cars ran thru to Los Angeles on the western end, terminating in San Diego, 2354-miles from its origin.

Vanishing Vistas®

Illustration: **The Chief**, eastbound
Location: Alray, California
Photo date: March 20, 1950

ATCHISON, TOPEKA AND SANTA FE RAILWAY

PHOTO BY CHARD L. WALKER—TEXT BY ROBERT A. LE MASSENA

TA-005-1-660:

Anyone who had witnessed Atchison, Topeka & Santa Fe railroad freight trains struggling upgrade on Cajon Pass in the era of steam-powered locomotion would have been astounded by this picture photographed in the summer of 1965, a decade after steam locomotives had made their final runs up the steep hill. The mechanical statistics of this scene are awesome indeed. Six diesel-electric locomotives, with a total of 30 driving axles and an aggregate engine-rating of nearly 15,000-horsepower, have been assigned to this freight train, which is drifting downgrade under the retarding influence of electro-dynamic braking, and without the usual accompanying cloud of bluish smoke emitted from the brake shoes beneath each car.

In order, the internal-combustion units are numbers 923, 968, 1225, 1398, 1345, and an unidentified 900-series member. The 900-series units (renumbered to the 4500-series in 1968) are GM-EMD SD24 models, 80 of which had been produced for the Santa Fe during 1959 and 1960, numbered 900 - 979. (Construction numbers were 25190 for the 923 and 25878 for the 968.) All of them have 2400-hp. engines, and they ride on two six-wheel, three-motor trucks (C-C arrangement). The 1200-series locomotives, numbered from 1200 thru 1284 (now 3200-series since 1968), are GM-EMD GP30 model units which had been produced during 1962 and 1963, using components from an equal number of early F-series units which had been traded in after two decades of useful service. For accounting purposes each new unit was considered to have been "rebuilt" from a specific older F-unit, though this distinction was not necessarily adhered to on the erection floor at La Grange. Thus, the 1225 was listed as having previously been a GM-EMD FT-model unit numbered 171C (construction number 3317) and built in 1945. In "re-incarnation," its 1350-hp. engine had been replaced by one of 2250-hp., while new or re-built generator and traction motors of appropriate capacity were installed. The 1389 and 1345 (construction numbers 30103 and 28742) were among 161 2500-hp. GP35-model units which had been derived in a similar manner from other former F-series units in 1964 and 1965.

The location of this picture is of more than superficial interest, being the point where the two separate lines up the south slope of Cajon Pass (north of San Bernardino, California) diverge. The original line (at the right) had been constructed in 1886, with the seven-mile segment from this point to the summit having a gradient of almost 3.5%, while that below was inclined at 2.3%. Additional traffic came to the pass in 1905 when the Union Pacific system (in the form of the San Pedro, Los Angeles & Salt Lake Railroad) negotiated operating rights with the Santa Fe to run its trains between Daggett (near Barstow) and Riverside (California). In 1913 a new line for upgrade trains (visible curving away to the left) was built on a separate nine-mile long alignment, with a maximum grade of "only" 2.3%, while those headed downhill continued to use the steeper track, as seen here. The station identification of this junction is Cajon (the crest of Cajon Pass is identified as Summit station), and from here on down into San Bernardino the two tracks lie side by side, in the manner of double track except for their "left-hand" running.

After a brief and unsatisfactory experiment with home-assembled Mallets, the Santa Fe used 2-10-2's almost exclusively on freight trains until 1941 when the first diesel-electrics began to arrive. By 1954 steam power was only a recent memory on the pass, and thereafter the multipled, rounded-nose units reigned supreme until they too were superseded by more powerful hood-unit locomotives like those in this picture.

Vanishing Vistas®

Illustration: EMD SD24 No. 923
Location: Cajon, California
Photo date: August 1965

ATCHISON, TOPEKA AND SANTA FE RAILWAY

SANTA FE RAILWAY PHOTO—TEXT BY ROBERT A. LE MASSENA

Photo by William H. Mills

In the latter half of the nineteenth century, the stature of a named train was measured by connotations of distant oceans or territories in its name. Indications of urgency and public service, like "Mail" and "Express," engendered esteem among travelers as the next century unfolded. In turn, these were superseded by names which had no connection at all with rail transport—Zephyr, Rocket, Chief. Despite these changes in nomenclature, the Atchison, Topeka & Santa Fe railroad retained one name which embodied the ultimate appeal—**Fast Mail Express**—which appeared in public timetables, along with **Super Chief, California Limited,** and **El Capitan**, until World War II years. Its disappearance did not mean that the train had been discontinued or that its schedule was no longer reliable; rather, its single coach did not provide the sort of accommodations to which the Santa Fe's patrons were accustomed to on other trains. The **Fast Mail Express** continued to accept passenger patronage, as did other long-distance mail trains on the AT&SF, although the lone car at the end of the train might have been a long way from the station, and the train itself running ahead of the times shown in employees' timetables.

The coming of super-fast streamlined trains, whose running times precluded delays involved in handling mail, baggage and express shipments at each stop, caused the concentration of head-end traffic into long solid consists, like the one shown in this picture. Their overall schedules were only slightly slower than those of the systems fastest trains, but point-to-point speeds were frequently much higher because of the great amount of time lost at station stops for handling the contents of the cars. In the days of steam motive-power, mail trains were pulled by the newest and best locomotives. After diesel-electric units superseded steam engines these non-passenger trains, as well as mainline passenger trains of secondary importance, were accorded different, but not inferior, treatment from the motive-power department. On the Santa Fe's far western end this policy translated into odd or older units—GM-EMD A1A-A1A E-series of 1800 or 2000 engine-horsepower, F-M ALT 100.3-models with 2000-horsepower engines and A1A-A1A trucks, or Alco PA/PB units, also with A1A-A1A trucks and 2000 engine-horsepower. Of these, the Alco units were the most numerous, there having been only three of the F-M units in all, and four of them, two cab-units followed by two booster-units, were hauling the westbound **Fast Mail Express** downgrade on the southern side of Cajon Pass when this picture was photographed.

With the exception of two experimental units (cab and booster) acquired in 1941, all of the Santa Fe's Alco passenger units were delivered in 1946 - 1948. However, the numbers of units 64 - 69 and 74 - 78 dated back to 1949, due to a renumbering at that time. Those 11 units had been delivered in 1947 and 1948, as the rear units of three-unit (cab-booster-cab) combinations, and their locomotive numbers received the Santa Fe's "B"-suffix, which meant "third unit" of a combination, 52B-62B. Because the third unit (booster) in four-unit locomotives also bore the "B"-suffix, there was no doubt some confusion among the railroad's personnel in identifying one of these Alco's. Consequently, they were renumbered, eliminating any uncertainty. The 66, thus had been produced as 54B, in 1947. Eventually, all of the Alco units were scrapped excepting four—59, 60, 62, 66—which were sold to the Delaware & Hudson railroad, becoming their No's. 16 - 19. These cab-units weighed 318,000 pounds, and could exert a tractive effort of 53,000 pounds.

In this scene the **Fast Mail Express** is passing through Blue Cut, just north of Keenbrook, where the canyon becomes quire narrow. Operations over the pass are left-hand, because the new uphill track, diverging from the steeper downhill one at Cajon, is located to the west of the original mainline.

Vanishing Vistas®

Illustration: **Fast Mail Express,**
      westbound
Location: Blue Cut, California
Photo date: June 4, 1967

ATCHISON, TOPEKA AND SANTA FE RAILWAY

PHOTO BY WILLIAM H. MILLS—TEXT BY ROBERT A. LE MASSENA

Photo by Gary G. Allen

The 128 mile line of the Atchison, Topeka & Santa Fe railroad between Los Angeles and San Diego was used as the final refuge of motive power which had been displaced from mainline duties. The gigantic 4-8-4's, of fast-freight and heavy-passenger fame, ran their last miles there, as did the early A1A-A1A diesel-electric units, first those built by GM, followed by Alco's machines. Eventually the railroad's passenger-service B-B units gravitated to that motive-power valhalla, but a shift of national transport policy brought them the prospect of extended but indefinite life.

When Amtrak took over the responsibility for operation of all long-distance passenger service in mid-1971, it purchased from various railroads their E8- and E9-model A1A-A1A diesel-electric locomotives, and late-production F7-model units equipped with train-heating equipment, a total of 423 units. An additional 74 B-B units were leased from the Santa Fe for operation between Chicago and San Diego over their home-line tracks. This arrangement was continued until new replacement units could be procured.

Ordinarily, the Santa Fe employed cab-booster-booster-cab groups, bearing identical road-numbers, to haul its passenger consists, but the 300-series locomotives were comprised of but one cab-unit and two boosters, the first of which were numbered 300, 300A, 300B - 316, 316A, 316B, all delivered between 1949 and 1951. Hense, by Amtrak standards, they were too old for continued service, except for secondary runs.

Three **San Diegan's** were scheduled each way daily on a schedule requiring just under three hours with five intermediate stops. This was one of the very few remaining routes over which more than two trains per day each way were operated. Two complete sets of equipment were used, requiring two pairs of units like the one pictured here.

San Diego (actually National City) was the Santa Fe's initial terminus on the Pacific Ocean. Using track material brought from Europe by ship, construction commenced in 1881 paralleling the coast line. The route turned inland and followed Temecula Canyon through the Santa Ana Mountains, as far as Colton on the Southern Pacific. The remaining gap—over Cajon Pass between San Bernardino and Barstow—was not completed until 1885, the result of legal and physical obstructions. Floods destroyed track in the canyon so often that a new line was constructed through Santa Ana at the northern end of the mountains, thence to Colton.

Strangely enough, this route along the ocean is not gradeless. Immediately upon departing San Diego trains ascend a 2.1% gradient in Rose Canyon to a summit at Miramar; then they descend a 2.2% gradient in Soledad Canyon to regain sea-level at Sorrento, 21 miles north of San Diego. On this stretch, the curves are so sharp that all trains are restricted to only 25 mph. In times past, helpers had been used on any freight trains which could not climb the hill, but recently the Santa Fe decided to eliminate mid-train diesel-electric helpers, thus requiring heavy freight trains to make two upgrade trips.

On this single-track line, increasing freight and passenger traffic is making it more difficult to operate more trains of both kinds, as well as to increase speeds. Consequently, there is talk of building a new high-speed passenger-only railroad, which would permit the operation of freight trains exclusively on the existing track.

Vanishing Vistas®

Illustration: **The San Diegan**
Location: San Diego, California
Photo date: February 10, 1973

ATCHISON, TOPEKA AND SANTA FE RAILWAY

PHOTO BY GARY G. ALLEN—TEXT BY ROBERT A. LE MASSENA

TA-005-1-1870:

The GM-EMD F45-model diesel-electric units, numbered 5900 - 5939 (originally numbered 1900 - 1939), are not truly a new variety of locomotive, despite their appearance which is quite different from that of their predecessors. Actually, they are SD45-model units, freight-service companions to the pioneer FP45-model, eight of which were produced in late 1967 for the **Super Chief—El Capitan**, whose customary motive power had been multipled GM-EMD F7-model units. Unlike the SD45-model units, however, these special ones have sloped and beveled surfaces relieving the rectangular severity of the standard configuration, and the engine-generator assemblage is housed, not in a close fitting hood, but in a cowled enclosure resembling that of the earlier E- and F- series units. In one important respect they differ: the cowl does not participate in any load-carrying construction, as did the housing of the E- and F- models. The Santa Fe had purchased ninety SD45-model units in 1966, then tried forty of the F45-model in 1968, but reverted to the standard SD45 design in 1969 and 1970, when 35 of them were added. At the time of their construction the FP45 units were the heaviest units on the railroad—412,000 pounds— and their tractive effort of 103,000 pounds was also the greatest, with but a single exception of six GE U30CG-model units having identical specifications.

The presence of two F45's and one SD45 at the head of a freight train attests to two characteristics of Santa Fe's operations: speed and grades. At this location, the train is running westbound near Williams (Arizona), and will coast for almost all of the 200 miles downhill to Needles (California) on the Colorado River, only 480 feet above sea-level. Between there and the Pacific Ocean are two summits with opposing grades of 1% to 1.5%. One is at Goffs (California), 2590 feet, the other being a choice of Cajon Pass, 3820 feet, or Tehachapi Pass, 3960 feet in elevation.

Santa Fe's east-west mainline—that part of it from Isleta (New Mexico), to Needles (California), is actually the railroad's second route to the West Coast, the first one having been part of the El Paso (Texas) branch (Isleta to Deming) thence over the Southern Pacific. Collaborating with the St. Louis-San Francisco railroad, the Atlantic & Pacific was constructed across northern Arizona to the Colorado River, where it met a newly-built line of the SP in 1883. In the following year the Santa Fe leased this trackage (Needles—Mojave), and obtained trackage rights over the SP into San Francisco. Then, in 1885, the Santa Fe reached the Pacific over its own track by constructing a line from Barstow over Cajon Pass to Colton, where it connected with an older line from San Diego. In time, the Santa Fe obtained the Needles—Mojave segment by exchanging it for the branch from Benson (Arizona), through Nogales and Hermosillo, to Guaymas, Mexico, on the Sea of Cortez.

This forest belt in an otherwise almost-treeless countryside is due to a long mountain chain forming the Arizona Divide, where rainfall is locally much heavier than on the surrounding semi-desert. The area has supported a thriving lumbering industry, with headquarters at Flagstaff. Many of the trees are very old, average ones dating back to the era of Columbus' voyages, while exceptional specimens are 100 years older.

Vanishing
Vistas®

Illustration: EMD F45 No. 5907
Location: Near Williams, Arizona
Photo date: September 1971

ATCHISON, TOPEKA AND SANTA FE RAILWAY

SANTA FE RAILWAY PHOTO—TEXT BY ROBERT A. LE MASSENA

Santa Fe Railway Photo

TA-005-1-3702:

Any eastbound Atchison, Topeka & Santa Fe railroad freight train, en route from the Pacific Coast to Chicago, had already surmounted two summits by the time it traversed the State of California and crossed the Colorado River into Arizona. If it originated in the San Francisco Bay Area, it climbed over Tehachapi Pass at 3930 feet above the sea, or over 3820 foot Cajon Pass had it come from the Los Angeles region. Furthermore, regardless of origin, it would have crossed over still another divide at Goffs (California), 2590 feet in altitude.

When the freight train pictured here left Topock (elevation less than 500 feet) at the California-Arizona border, it faced still another formidable challenge. Ahead was one of the longest grades on any North American railroad. Commencing at Topock, the rails climbed a 1.4% grade to a summit at Louise, 52 miles distant and 3000 feet higher. After a 12 mile easy descent to Walapai, the 1.4% grade continued to another summit at Yampai, gaining another 2200 feet elevation in 50 miles. Twenty miles east of Walapai was Crozier Canyon, the location of this photo taken in 1976. From Yampai to the Arizona Divide at Riordan (7300 feet elevation, and fifty feet higher than the Continental Divide at Gonzales, New Mexico) lay 100 miles of sawtooth profile with a twenty mile stretch of 1.8% gradient. (This difficult segment was subsequently by-passed between Williams and Crookton with a lesser-gradient relocated line.)

The two GE U36C diesel-electric units leading two unidentified GM-EMD units on the point of this long freight train represent the most recent development in that category of internal-combustion locomotion since the first ones arrived in 1939. Sixty-four of these powerful locomotives, with 3600-horsepower engines and C-C trucks, were received in 1974 and 1975 to help handle fast mainline freight traffic.

Competing with the Southern Pacific and Union Pacific systems, both of which have more favorable profiles, though longer routes, between California and the Midwest, the Santa Fe's transportation task is far from easy. Once the SP and UP trains cross California's eastern boundary, the remainders of their long runs are comparatively easy, but for the Santa Fe the most difficult part lies ahead of the four diesel-electrics in this scene.

This entire 460 mile stretch of double-track mainline, between Barstow (California), and Winslow (Arizona), presented extreme difficulties for the operation of steam locomotives. Water and fuel-oil had to be hauled to several points, and the long grades required extra stops to cool car wheels which had become overheated by continuous braking. Moreover, helper districts were unusually lengthy, and uphill freight train speeds were agonizingly slow. Consequently, at the very end of 1940, the Santa Fe commenced to replace steam power with GM-EMD FT-model diesel-electric units, which initially were assigned to this particular region to prevent what could have been a very serious bottleneck during World War II.

The railroad's original route to the Pacific Coast had been one which extended south from Albuquerque (New Mexico), then westward across southern Arizona to a connection with the Southern Pacific at Deming (New Mexico). Not wishing to be blocked by the SP in its ambitions to reach ocean ports, the Santa Fe backed the Atlantic & Pacific in the construction of a new mainline across northern Arizona. This track met that of the SP at Needles (California), across the Colorado River from Topock. After leasing this SP track for a couple of years, the Santa Fe acquired it in an exchange, and was then able to attain its goal at San Diego, California.

Vanishing Vistas®

Illustration: GE U36C No. 8773
Location: Crozier Canyon,
            Arizona
Photo date: June 1976

ATCHISON, TOPEKA AND SANTA FE RAILWAY

SANTA FE RAILWAY PHOTO—TEXT BY ROBERT A. LE MASSENA